Effective Entrepreneurial Action

For Beginners and Beyond

James Regan

Income Disclaimer

This document contains business strategies, marketing methods and other business advice that, regardless of my own results and experience, may not produce the same results (or any results) for you. I make absolutely no guarantee, expressed or implied, that by following the advice below you will make any money or improve current profits, as there are several factors and variables that come into play regarding any given business.

Primarily, results will depend on the nature of the product or business model, the conditions of the marketplace, the experience of the individual, and situations and elements that are beyond your control.

As with any business endeavor, you assume all risk related to investment and money based on your own discretion and at your own potential expense.

Liability Disclaimer

By reading this document, you assume all risks associated with using the advice given below, with a full understanding that you, solely, are responsible for anything that may occur as a result of putting this information into action in any way, and regardless of your interpretation of the advice.

You further agree that myself as an author, or our company cannot be held responsible in any way for the success or failure of your business as a result of the information presented below. It is your responsibility to conduct your own due diligence regarding the safe and successful operation of your business if you intend to apply any of our information in any way to your business operations.

I am not a financial adviser and any financial decisions of any significance should always be first consulted with your financial representative, CPA, or Lawyer. These concepts and ideas presented are primarily for educational use. Your decision to act upon these concepts are in fact your decision and your responsibility, as results of course will vary from individual to individual.

Terms of Use

You are given a non-transferable, "personal use" license to this product. You cannot distribute it but you *can* share the concepts with other individuals verbally or in a training session. Also, there are no resale rights or private label rights granted when purchasing this document.

Effective Entrepreneurial Action

For Beginners and Beyond

Table of Contents

Benefits from reading this book: 9
Acknowledgements: 11
Chapter 1 13
Why is it so important to be *an*
Effective Entrepreneur? 13
Chapter 2 *Moving from Dreams to Sweet*
Success..21
Chapter 3...31
What does it *Actually Take to be Successful in*
Business? 31
Chapter 4...45
The Bottom line of Effective
Entrepreneurial *Action*.................................45
Chapter 5 *The Eight Secrets of Effective*
Entrepreneurial Thinking...............................49
Chapter 6...59
The Key Elements of Executive Action.............59
Chapter 7 Exciting Post *Executive Activities*.....67
Chapter 8...73
Why not build *yourself a Bank?*.......................73
Chapter 9...87
The End, or should I say,*The Beginning* 87
Bibliography 91
About The Author...97

Benefits from reading this book:

-In step by step format obtain the ability to distinguish between the mindsets that will facilitate success in business, as opposed to the mindsets that don't.

-*Find out from a practical stand point the specific key elements needed to be successful as an entrepreneur, whether the business is traditional, online, or through networks, such as affiliate and network marketing.*

-Incorporate the key traits of an Executive and employ those values into your own lifestyle.
-*Learn how to set up an effective itinerary for your life's ambitions, dreams, or goals.*

-Understand what makes an Entrepreneur effective, as opposed to one being not so effective.
-*Learn about a poorly understood but very effective tool to reduce one's personal tax liability.*

-Discover the simple method of (Combined Asset Building) as a means to keep afloat in this shaky economy.

Bonus Chapter -*Utilize the asset building techniques to mimic the actions of a bank, as if the bank was yours!*

Acknowledgements:

I would first like to thank my dear wife Miriam. We have come through a lot of situations together, and have come through them all. I know it takes a lot of patience and fortitude to be an author's wife. Let many years of good things come upon us, that we can continue to help more people as we grow.

I also would like to thank Brandon Horton my chief editor. I love to watch how you think, as you polish the manuscript into something much greater than it was. I enjoy the times when we get together and discuss the many subjects that we do. Those times are always fun.

I also would like to take the time to thank my mother, Ardath Regan. You have always been a model of courage, daring, diligence, and entrepreneurship for me. You led Holly, Michigan well as mayor, you brought Holly's history into life, and you helped build many young lives up with Frank, as a team in the Optimist Club. You showed by example that there are really no obstacles or boundaries in life, just the one's people set for themselves or limit themselves to. Your legacy will be remembered in the memories of all of the people's lives that you've touched. This book again is written in dedication and honor to you.

I would also like to acknowledge the book cover's final design to pixel studio. You did a great job on it, and thanks.

To all others who have been a personal support or perhaps a listening ear, I thank you. Sometimes you don't realize who and how valuable your support system is until it gets tested.

Chapter 1

Why is it so important to be an Effective Entrepreneur?

In this day and age, amidst the new economy, most of us find ourselves considerably troubled by what is happening to our financial infrastructure. If you are an employee thinking about becoming an entrepreneur or you are an entrepreneur already, this uneasiness is most likely due to the fact that you have recognized the inadequacy of your own income being able to fully meet your needs. You may have also realized that your future income needs, including your retirement needs, have been poorly or completely left unaddressed.

You have come to this conclusion because, even though you have fought to save some of your income, the *expense demand* on your personal finances remains consistent. It pulls, it tugs, it sucks, and it drains at your reserves until finally it begins to eat away at your personal hope and internal stamina. You watch your dreams slowly erode away as these invisible leeches continue to feed off of your financial and psychological resolve.

First of all, before we go any farther, I want to congratulate you in the recognition of this condition. Many people, sadly, don't see it at all. They are resigned and therefore confined to their mediocre and sometimes monotonous routines. They get up, very early, work all day, commute home, arrive tired and befuddled, perhaps even depressed. In many cases they just want to entirely forget their day. They become quickly immersed in family affairs, favorite T.V. shows, movies, video games, perhaps a book, or even Facebook, etc. There is nothing wrong to say about any of these activities, for they provide plentiful enjoyment, like therapeutic salve bringing the distractive relief to the sores and pains of the day.

So take heart because you do perceive these routines and inadequacies. They are accurate perceptions on your part in their inability to sustain your future by themselves, which many still do not see. Some do feel it but can't quite put their finger on what's going on. Yet it has not moved them enough to do something about it to find their way out of this financial cage. Not so with you.

But then, what are these financial leeches that deplete our hope and what makes up this hidden cage of our economy that makes it clear that we need to become self-sufficient and entrepreneurial. That is if we intend to get ahead, let alone survive. Let's take a look at them, shall we?

First U.S. Mint Building-Philadelphia, PA.

First and foremost, we have to take a very slight peek into what makes up our economy, how it ticks, in order to understand how it affects us. Once we understand this, then we can take effective action in order to change the things we wish to change. Of course, I am speaking to those of us who are awake and not asleep, like you.

The general infrastructure starts with the government, (which was just recently shut down), in how it manages its finances and how we are taxed. There is also the Federal Reserve, which is a private corporation and <u>not</u> a governmental entity. It is important to note how it interacts with the government and other major banks and how it controls the actual throttles and brakes of our economy.

More specifically, the Federal Reserve and Federal Government interact back and forth through the buying and selling of different kinds of financial notes and instruments such as: T-Bills, treasury notes, bonds, etc. This is done in huge quantities and therefore whatever interest is earned can be substantial.[1]

The Federal Reserve simultaneously also interacts with the Mega-Banks either via loans and deposits. Again, the amount of money involved in each transaction is substantial. These day by day loans are quite short, but again, the interest involved can produce hearty returns on their investment for the banks. Banks are also legally required to keep a certain amount of funds, held as reserves, which sets up this back and forth cash flow between the Federal Reserve and the larger banks. The Federal Reserve loans money at the *Federal Funds rate* [2] directly influences the Mega-Banks to set their *Prime Rate* interest rates. [3]

This establishes the next level of interest rates for the medium and smaller banks called the *discount rate*. These in turn is who interact with us, the public, set the interest rates for car loans, house loans, etc., based off of but higher than the prime rate. So in effect you can see how the Federal Reserve indirectly and directly has a hand in the speeding up or the slowing down of our economy by adjusting the interest rates. For instance, we have observed the now up-swinging interest rates in the Real Estate Market, yet just prior to this upswing the interest rates were being dropped. This is so more loans could be started, to make more money move and speed up the economy. In order to slow the process down you would have to raise the interest rates instead.

The Federal Government itself also directly has a means to control the raising and lowering of our taxes. The raising of taxes in effect slows our purchasing down, while the lowering of taxes allows us to continue spending the same or even more so. These interest and taxation controls, amongst other factors, affect our cost of living through what's known as the CPI or *Consumer Price Index*. The Consumer Price Index is determined by comparing groups of foods across several points in the country, ultimately producing an average cost figure for those same groups of foods. The Consumer Price Index can also be affected when the Federal Reserve prints new money and places it into the economy system. [4]

This in effect dilutes the overall money and thus what a dollar buys today may be $1.10 tomorrow. This is how inflation works and why we then get raises at our jobs just to keep pace with the cost of living. (This process is meant to stimulate the economy if it's handled correctly). Sometimes money will be taken out of the system to reverse the process, but if you were to measure inflation through the decades you would see it rising in a fairly consistent manner.

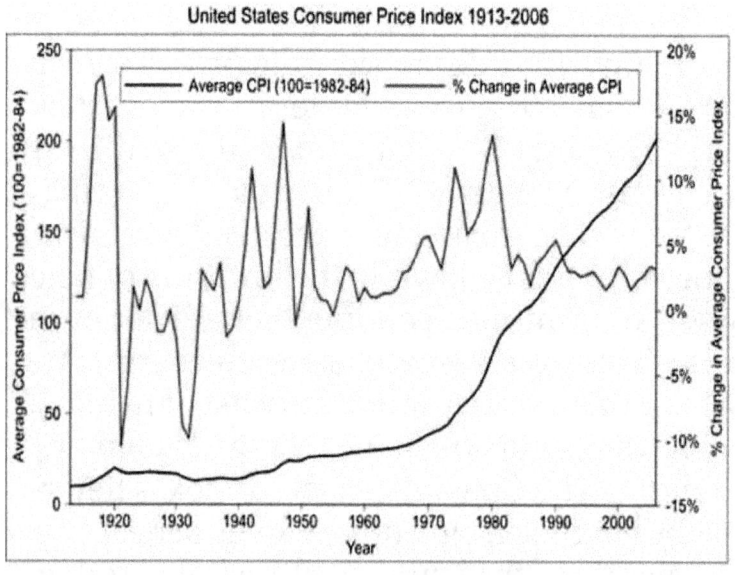

So here we are as employees, trying to make ends meet, watching the cost of living going up like an endless upward spiral? Even if you work enough overtime, you don't get what you think you would get, based on the new tax level you now get taxed from because you made that extra income. Our raises too, end up pinching us just a little more for tax at the end of the year, because our income goes up slightly because of the raise. We have to see things from the taxation point of view.

But wait, what about sales tax for when we buy things, ie; gas tax, cigarette tax, tax here, tax there, tax even the underwear. With all of these things going on and inflation on the rise, how can anyone get ahead of this? The truth is, as an employee it's very difficult, almost impossible. There are some I know that are even playing to the tune of three jobs, just to make ends meet.

Now we can decline and resign ourselves to all of this and just try to enjoy our life the best we can or we can look for a way to overcome these dynamics. In order for the Wright Brothers to overcome the problem of flight they had to understand the physical dynamics of gravity, lift, and other factors. Once they understood, though trial and error they eventually overcame the aero-dynamics of that system. So, if we begin to educate ourselves and understand the essential dynamics of what's keeping us chained up in this money system, then and only then can we apply the same kind of overcoming principles to our personal situation and begin to financially fly.

That is exactly what the entrepreneur is all about. Now the question is, how can we effectively take entrepreneurial action, so that it does not necessarily require one to have a financial degree? What steps can one take so that they can know that they are heading in the right direction?

Chapter 2 Moving from Dreams to Sweet Success

Now this is where it gets interesting. This is where you take your dreams and begin making them a reality. I am sure most of us desire our dreams to become reality but if you think about it from beginning to end, that could be quite a tall order for some. Not an impossible order, just a tall one. Why is that? Because a dream is just a dream until you put legs on it. Meaning our desires, wishes, hopes, and dreams are fabulous when we think about them, but when we actually set our minds to go after them something else happens inside.

They end up looking so far away. They seem noble, but farfetched. The actuality of those goals becoming true could be slim to none. Some give up right there. Others start pursuing, but it still seems a far way off even after they have genuinely given themselves over to it, because "hope that is deferred can make the heart sick." [5] It can finally make one give up.

So how do we truly move from our dreams to sweet success? Even before answering this how many of you have really dedicated some personal quiet time to discover what your true deep down desires are for your life, and what legacy you would like to leave behind you? Let's put first things first.

If you don't have the time now, stop here, until the next reading. If you do have some time you can invest now for yourself, I want you to right now get a piece of paper or notebook and start thinking about these desires and dreams you've had but life got in the way. It would be like the list you have mentally made and talked about with others if you won the lottery and never needed to worry about finances again. This will take some time. It could take up to a couple of hours to do it. It's uncomfortable.

The reason it will take some time is that after you win that kind of money and have vacationed a bit, bought a house for your family members, and perhaps helped out a few friends, you begin to get more serious about it and think of how you can put the multitudinous leftover lottery winnings to good use. You begin to think of your personal desires that you want for yourself and your family. Go ahead, list them out now. You might think about things you want to do like opening a personal recording studio or art center. Perhaps you want to start a foundation or start some other means of helping people. Maybe you want to own a hunting ranch, or maybe you want to invest it in a way that you could live off the interest for good.

Your desires are your desires. Only you can dig them up out of yourself like silver and gold being mined up out of the ground. Take the time to list them now. You are worth the investment. You do not have to fill out all of the lines here, they are there for you if you need them. If you prefer to write them somewhere else that is fine. You must decide, however, to do this just for you, because you want them, not because I suggest that you do them for you. It has to be coming truly from you.

<u>Desire Action List</u>

1.

_____

2.

_____

3.

_____

4.

_____

5.

_____

6.

_____

7.

_____

8.

_____

9.

_____

10.

_____

11.

_____

12.

_____

13.

_____

14.

_____

15.

_____

Congratulations! You have accomplished a big step. If you've got your desires written out on paper as instructed you are going to feel a whole lot better. If you find yourself wanting to skip this, ask yourself why? Perhaps you have lost your feelings for your dreams and you find it difficult to dream at all. Write them down anyway. Write what you want and perhaps what you don't want. You will feel better when you do, as you will begin to see how important your dreams really are. It is because your personal dreams and desires in this life have a lot to do with the deeper side of you. They are real things and that is why when your hopes are deferred or put off enough they begin to eat away at the real you and make the heart sick.

Now that you have gotten your dreams written down, you can do something concrete about them. They are no longer floating around in your head abstract and aloof, as they have been, surfacing from time to time to remind you that they are still there. Instead they are affixed, they are distinctly written down. There is a saying in an ancient manuscript that states:

"Write the vision down, make it plain upon tablets, that he may run that reads it." 7

Now, because your dreams have been precipitated into something tangible, you can move towards them, actually accomplishing them. How do you start doing this? You can memorize them, you can recite them, you can look at them, plan them, etc. In Napoleon Hill's book, *Think and Grow Rich*, he discusses the term "affirmations" where you keep affirming by reading and speaking these goals over your life knowing they will eventually come to pass.7 These affirmations are proclamations of your long range goals, your targets, and mental prods that move you from being a dreamer to someone actually walking out their reality.

Just think about how you felt when you accomplished one of your biggest goals. Did you not feel victorious? Did you not feel great? This is how you will feel when your dreams get legs and begin to walk. By getting legs I mean after converting a dream to a long range goal, a real target, and a real destination. *"A desire that is fulfilled is sweet to the soul."* 8

When I go on a driving trip with my family, I enjoy planning out our itinerary ahead of time. I look at how many days I have and then estimate the mileage I will travel each day. I plan candidate routes that appear to be scenic, and I look for vacation hotspots like Yosemite Park, Lake Tahoe, or Ventura Beach. They have become my little goals.

If I want to go from Dallas to D.C. to visit the Capitol, I can use a map to measure how far I have come and how far I have yet to go. I can use major cities as reference points to track my progress. In the same way you can track your progress towards your real long range goals and

26

dreams by breaking up your journey into chewable bites. How do you do that? You break up your long range goals into several smaller goals. By doing this the dream or desire that looks almost impossible as a whole, now looks not so far away because they have been broken up into accomplishable pieces. Your dream has now become more believable and feasible.

Let's say you have a desire or dream to become a great pianist. If you're young enough, the first place to start is taking music lessons and then become part of the school's band or orchestra. You learn about written notes and how they connect to the actual music that is played. Perhaps later you take college courses in music to further your skills. You pick the style of music you wish to play or learn multiple styles and instruments. Then you enter competitions or connect up with a band to further your experience and skills. You then start looking to cut an album and get sponsored by someone who now believes in your skills and then all of a sudden you are cutting songs like "Piano Man" by Billy Joel.

You begin to outdo those around you. You create something better like Bill Gates or Steve Jobs did. Whatever your goal is you keep moving towards it with persistence and accountably, measuring your progress until you finally arrive at your sweet destination of success. If you fail like Edison did, it's Ok. He stumbled along, failing hundreds of times before he obtained his goal of creating a workable and usable filament for the light bulb.

You don't stop to complete your trip in Atlanta when you are on your way to Washington D.C. from Dallas. You can stop temporarily, just for a rest, but you keep going until you arrive. Once you start moving on your journey you may even rewrite, stretch, and recalibrate your goals to something better than what you originally planned. This is because you see where you are going now and your perspectives may have changed as you move. Because they change many times your goals get readjusted to reach higher heights. That's because you are now believing better.

No one else will get you there but you. There are many around you who have not yet personally formulated their dreams and could unconsciously or even consciously attempt to dissuade you, deciding for you what you can accomplish or what you cannot accomplish. How do they know? They might mean well or may be joking but if they get you to buy into their thinking they might just actually get you to give up on your dreams.

People like this can be like crabs in a basket. If a crab sees another crab trying to escape the basket he can grab on to the escaping crab's leg just to bring him back down into the crowd of crabs, that believe they have no hope of escape. They even feel better after they have helped you come to your senses and become more realistic about life like them.

A couple of movies to watch that distinctly display this battle, using true to life characters, who did not stop fighting for their dreams in the midst of great opposition are: <u>Rudy</u> and <u>The Pursuit of Happiness</u>. In both of these movies you will experience their struggle, feel their focus, and become inspired as you walk through their circumstances with them.

You will experience with them their eventual breakthrough via their rising above what others thought of them and what others did to them. These characters stayed on course until they finally got to where they originally had set their mind to go. They valued their dream and kept it continually in front of them, holding it high in priority, and walking doggedly resolute. They would not let circumstances or others stop them, no matter what.

There is an occurrence like this in the Bible, where a person named Jacob actually wrestled with an angel. Like a bulldog with a bone his response was, "I am not letting go until you bless me." If your desire is reasonable, obtainable, feasible and right, ***don't*** you dare let go.

The obtainment of dreams that are pursued is not always easy. They do not arrive on a silver platter. Many times they can involve even a difficult struggle. This is why a lot of people miss it. This is where they exit the highway!

Chapter 3

What does it Actually Take to be Successful in Business?

At this point I believe that you can see that it could take a lot of persistence and stamina. Many people that pursue their dreams, do not take this into account and what it will personally cost them. What I mean by that is what it will cost in terms of persistence, sacrifice, and yes, what it might mean financially, as far as the investment toward their goals. Many will start toward their dream, but as soon as they get on the road they begin to suddenly realize the work that is involved.

They begin to see that being an entrepreneur is actually harder than just being an employee, which is hard enough. This is because now as an entrepreneur, **the boss** of themselves has to tell **the employee** of themselves, that it's time to get to work. They either continue to persist and overcome their fears or eventually give up. They finally conclude that the cost of their goals is too much for them. They slowly talk themselves out of it and go back to the safe routines of the crab basket, justifying their actions, and why they are giving up on themselves and their own desires. Some attempt to try something else but arrive at the same place because this is their stopping point. They can't seem to make it past Atlanta.

There are reasons for this. In the books, *Rich Dad Poor Dad* and *The Cash Flow Quadrant,* Robert Kiyosaki clearly explains how there are four separate and unique areas that money moves in. He named it the "ESBI Quadrant." Making money as an **E**-mployee, as opposed creating income **S**-elf employed, as opposed to a **B**-ig business owner, or finally as an **I**-nvestor. He teaches how each quadrant has a different way of thinking and different rules that are associated with it, meaning a Big Business owner might approach the same problems differently than an employee would. People as employees like things safe, secure, predictable and dependable. [9]

Now this is where I would like to add something here. I believe that the E in the Cash Flow Quadrant not only can represent the employee, but can also simultaneously incorporate, mindset wise, the word; ***Entitlement.*** This is so, because entitlement has a certain mentality associated with it as well. Yet unlike E for employee, which is associated primarily with the making of income, entitlement can extend beyond the work place, playing into many parts of one's life.

In the online version of Merriam Webster dictionary, the definition of entitlement means "the belief that one is deserving or entitled to a certain privilege." "The condition of the right to have, the right to do, or get something." [10] Now in a lot of ways that seems good. But many are taking this idea further than what is supposed to mean. It is partly due to our surrounding culture that we find ourselves in today. In this fast food, fast paced, information age, a lot of us plainly believe that we deserve to have things conveniently laid out for us. This has come through many years of conditioning.

Our forefathers in this country farmed, worked, and established themselves through blood, through sweat, and through their many tears. Are we not just riding the wave of this great convenience, upon their lees? Think of how we're enjoying the conveniences of electricity, cars, refrigerators, freezers, air conditioning, airplanes, phone service, email, radio, T.V., and the Internet, and more. They lived their lives with none of those conveniences. They had to get up early, work hard, and struggle long hours just to get the food on the table for the family. Life was more physical back then. The work mentality and work ethics were very different. They could not digest an entitlement mentality, instead they vivaciously had an establishment mentality. They constructed things.

33

If they didn't do it who would? Ronald Reagan said, "If not us, who, if not now, when?" and President Kennedy said, "It's not what your country can do for you, but what you can do for your country." These two statements clearly reflect the conflict between the two mentalities. Sadly, the establishment mentality has slowly but surely been routed and eroded away by the entitlement mentality, which has become quite formidable. It is a mentality that could very well be the root of our country's unraveling. It will most certainly unravel one's inner fight with respect to obtaining their dreams.

I remember going to a business convention where Guiliani, a post New York City mayor, spoke about his own personal struggles, as he fought to change this kind of mentality in New York. He specifically had found that people who worked in the welfare department were actually getting incentives to get more people on welfare. This meant that they would get more bonuses relative to how many welfare accounts they personally would set up.

Though his ideas were unpopular, he was determined to change the welfare system. He did not deny people who needed the help, but now the incentives were turned around. They were turned around in respect to those individuals on welfare. They would still receive welfare but had to get help and support so they would get a job and eventually get freed from that welfare support, totally, and come to a place of supporting themselves.

I saw this as a very healthy and appropriate solution. It provided ways to help those in need but phased down on those who wanted to remain in this state of mind, especially if they could get out of it. He fought against the entitlement system and turned it into a proactive system. He provided support, but with a way out. When people originally came to this country, they came to the land of opportunity and hope, not to the land of ease, and lean on me.

Similarly, when one personally looks at the obtainment of their goals there needs to be a shift from any of this residual entitlement inside of themselves to a state of being proactive as Steven Covey explains clearly in his book, *The Seven Habits of Highly Successful People.* He points out that some people react to situations blaming others for their circumstances, where those who proactively look at their situations are in the personal expectation mode of overcoming. They determine their own paths by becoming accountable. They are accountable for themselves and to themselves, and also accountable to others.[11]

Overcoming entitlement in oneself is one of the first steps in obtaining your goals because they are "*your*" goals and yours alone. Therefore, it's up to you and no one else to obtain them. Yes, working with a team can help get you there but just depending on a team with an entitlement mindset will not. Many network marketers fail here, because they genuinely work for a while, but then shift to an entitlement mentality. They expect their team to activate and do, while the team is expecting their leader to help them to get them where they want to go. All this is true but if entitlement and dependency is embedded within the equation it will fail. So the point to come away with here is that if you want to reach your goals, entitlement has to be weeded out.

In moving towards your dreams you now will have to monetize your goals. What does that mean? Depending on your desires or dream you have to make an estimate or real budget amount, as to what you think the lifestyle you are moving toward is going to cost. If you want to drive a Mercedes or live in a 6 bedroom house with a pool, library, and acres of land to boot, how much will the bill be? If you plan to own a movie studio and make movies, what will it take? What are its expenses? When big companies make business plans, that is exactly what they are do-ing is counting the cost, projecting their future gains, with the aim of giving a prospective inves-tor a reason to invest.

So now, the **second assignment:** Take your list and attach a financial amount to it and after doing it with each individual dream add up each cost, e.g.; traveling around the world, and then add it all up together to see what it will take to get there. Getting there is not only taking ac-count of the dream, but taking also into the account the cost. While initially this might be discouraging, you will get a more accurate picture in what your dreams are going to actually take in terms of persistence and cost.

Now that you have this done, how do we get there? Don't say "I can't afford it" say, "How can I afford it?" [12] If in your mind you believe that you have to stay within certain boundaries then so you shall. If however, in your mind you are looking to stretch your boundaries, as opposed to a stagnant state of *Que Sera, Sera*, accepting whatever comes your way, you automatically will begin to look for new possibilities. Open doors arise as opposed to just accepting your lot in life. One might even go as far as to nourish the victim mentality inside themselves in the attempt to foster sympathy from others justifying their entitlement to things.

I am not ignoring or being heartless towards those that genuinely might need our help but can you see how these kinds of mindsets can interfere with someone who attempts to expand themselves entrepreneurial wise, starting a real business?

Here is another saying that says, "As a man thinks, so is he."[13]

That sounds like you become the reality of what you think and then believe for yourself. It appears that we can create our own personal mental cage, or we can roam free with our lives on a fun adventure on a safari. From this saying it seems that it's showing us that we can literally set our own boundaries which can be very limited, or we can set them to almost be limitless. It's up to us.

To this I will also add here, that what other people think of us and how we perceive that can have effect on how we think, and so we are. The truth is when it comes down to the rubber meeting the road it is we ourselves, and how we think about things that has the greatest influence on ultimately determining our outcome and subsequently our income. Therefore this is good news because that means I can choose to look for the door and walk through it, if I want to. I don't have to stay in my cage that has been prescribed by myself or others.

Therefore when we look now at the comparison between someone who safely dwells in the employee mentality, even if they are a good one, will play it by the book, give proper deference to their boss, take less chances, avoid mistakes because adhering to this way of thinking provides the safety of a steady income, or so we think. Entrepreneurial thought is more creative, it takes greater chances, thinks outside of the box, and is not worried about making mistakes, for mistakes can actually hone your skills.

When I worked with two other partners in New York City as a professional carpet cleaner, we came up with the name for our business called, <u>Emerald</u> <u>Floors</u>. That business is still thriving today but only one of the original three contractors is still working there. I remember in the earliest of my days, when we established the company, that no one told me what I had to do, as I had already been trained what to do by another company. I knew what specific actions I had to take if I wanted to create business and see success for myself.

What do you think that was? Think it through a bit and give it a guess, it is not that difficult. The answer is that I had to find a way to promote what I was offering. I had to get the word out and advertise in some way. I had to create business cards, flyers, and then go out and talk to people, hand out fliers, and visit restaurants and other businesses. I had to follow up, make appointments, and close jobs. I had to make it happen myself. No one told me what I should or should not do. Compare this to the employee's mentality.

So an effective entrepreneur recognizes that if he wants to expand his territory, and stretch his boundaries it *will* take more work at first, and perhaps be more stressful because you are trying to establish something new and make it work.

Why do I say this? It is because employees trade time and talent for pay. Entrepreneurs trade time and talent at first similarly but in time they will surpass the employee in income, because an employee is bound to the time-clock and the whims of his or her employer, whereas an entrepreneur can actually get to the place where his or hers business can run itself creating profit and capital, whether the owner is there or not. That's how franchises work. Franchises have owners but are run primarily by managers and teenagers and people in their early 20s. The owners just check in from time to time and collect on their assets- positive cash flow.

These entrepreneurs have employees of their own and unlike employees they can take advantage of the many legal and legitimate tax deductions that can be enjoyed by those who know how to utilize them properly. The government recognizes that businesses create jobs, which creates more income, which creates more taxes for them. Predominately the tax code a, all 7500 pages of it are written as incentives for business owners rather than the employee. Therefore everyone should endeavor to start a business, just on this basis alone, as it will open these deduction doors. Even if your business is marketing toothpicks in a toy store or popsickles in Antartica, a business will end up saving you more money.

An employee who makes $50,000 gets taxed before he even touches it. He then goes out to buy things such as cell phones, Internet, Office Supplies, clothing, gas, food, etc. In comparison a business owner makes his $50k, then purchases the same kind of things but now can deduct those same items either partially or in full. It's the same amount of $50k in dollars but producing quite different outcomes, because businesses have those tax advantages. For instance 25k of the 50k might go towards expenses and the person who has a home based business or traditional business will then be taxed on just 25k rather than 50k.

Now is entrepreneurialism easy? No, not at first, but it is more fun because you feel you have more say and finances in your life than you do as an employee. You do not have to give up your employee job, but you can work your way out of an employee job little by little until the income you make part time supersedes the income you make as an employee full time. You can use your part time business to bankroll and monetize your dreams. Watch your dreams begin to grow legs quickly and walk towards your reality.

You can work with other partners and network with other people and build teams if you so desire, but you first must be resolved in your mind what the cost of time and money will be invested into your endeavor to get the ball rolling. If you tippy toe as an entrepreneur, you might as well not go this way, because to change your financial foundation and infrastructure to something better than you have now will take more effort and more work than what you're doing now. If you do decide to truly commit to yourself and work at it, then you can create the momentum in your business to effectually change things in your personal life, for good.

So this is what I mean by effective entrepreneur. Effective means to do, to accomplish, and to arrive at one's goal. It's a whole different way of thinking than an employee. I had to take many no's in carpet cleaning before I got a yes. The no's did hurt my feelings and I did not like it, but I forgot about the no's when I heard the yes.

That's what the entrepreneurial struggle is all about. It is going through the uncomfortable no's to get to the yes. By yes, of course, we are attempting to help people in their lives with what we have to offer. We are not trying to sell them or push them into them giving us their money; we are trying to help that person in their life with our products or services, whatever the particular business that we get involved with, by truly making their lives a little better through what we have to offer. We then, as a reward for this, get paid for our products or services rendered. We do it genuinely so we can be seen as a person who is sincerely committed to their benefit.

As an employee, unless driven by management, you do not necessarily have to satisfy the customer. You do not necessarily have to satisfy your co-workers or boss. For many employees work just enough not to get fired but they do not perform at their full creativity potential. As an entrepreneur you don't get paid until your customer or client has been satisfied. See the different mentality required to work effectively and efficiently as an entrepreneur?

Imagine if a regular worker worked at this level of proficiency how fast they would get promoted up the corporate ladder because of their relative diligence in comparison with the average worker. Unfortunately, there just isn't the same incentive for an employee to consistently work at this level of proficiency. If you are building someone else's business working by the hour rather than getting paid for what is produced, you will produce less; it's only natural.

If a person is willing to accept the time sacrificed, the effort spent, the books of self-improvement that might be needed to be read to effect those changes, then yes, you will effectually establish your business, get it rolling, and keep it rolling. You will eventually turn a profit, which can be a potentially substantial and consistent profit. If one recognizes from the get-go that it may take a few years, even up to five, to get over the hump towards a business that produces steady cash flow, ***then and only then***, are you in the right state of mind to weather the challenges that may become obstacles towards the reaching of your dreams.

This is the mindset that will produce success. It is an inward tenacity and bull-doggedness towards your goals and dreams that will bust through all the negatives, setbacks, disappointments, and course corrections that you might have to make in the pursuit of your dreams. This secret is the main essential ingredient towards the procuring of your success. The next step is taking your business from an establishment and production level to an automated state, where the business can run with you or without you. Once you achieve automation you achieve a cash flow that is now in a constant flow state like a river that never run's dry. It is then that you will begin to effectuate your dreams and become free enough to enjoy them.

Why don't we then look into this bottom line, a bottom line that will move us more into a continual line of success- After you!

Chapter 4

The Bottom line of Effective Entrepreneurial Action

When you think of the word effective you might also think of words like effectual, efficiency, and ethics too. Therefore true effectiveness will have efficiency incorporated within it. So in our quest to understand these key elements we will examine efficiency, effectiveness, and ethics side by side. First let's look at their definitions and see what we can observe.

Effective - "Having an intended or expected effect. Productive or capable of producing a result." [14]

Efficient - "Being effective without wasting time, effort, or expense." [15]

Ethics - "A set of moral principles containing right conduct. The moral fitness of a decision and course of action." [16]

The three words above; effective, efficient and ethics, say quite a *mouthful!* You can easily see that effective entrepreneurial action contains just that, productive action. It's not about the talking, it's not about the training, it's not about the meeting- *it's about the doing*, but doing it concisely and precisely. It is action that is simple, and direct, action that is without dilly-dallying. Results therefore are produced, whether they are in the area of money, time, or effort. It sounds like an effective entrepreneur groves while he moves, is with them in his rhythm, he gets them with momentum, and does not tire, because he's on fire.

It's like a hockey player or basketball player that finds his spot in the zone. Nothing seems to <u>not</u> work. All his moves are smooth, and his timing is impeccable. He's prepared and practiced. He sharply weaves in and out and around his obstacles. He dazzles and befuddles his opponents and then suddenly, he scores again.

He does all this, while he respects the other players around him, especially his teammates. He greatly respects the one whom he's serving, that is his customer. He finds it appalling when he sees other players taking short cuts, doing little fouls to get ahead rather than by good play. It's like it's a sneak-cheat. When one breaks the rules, callously hurting people, while they attempt to personally get ahead, even if it's done unwittingly, may ultimately take the wind out of their own sails. Bottom line- they might grow some but never into greatness. How can they?

Here is another powerful saying:

"An athlete is not crowned unless he competes according to the rules."[17]

True entrepreneurial executives remain and maintain a high level of ethics because they believe in doing things right and doing people right. That's when true prosperity occurs, not before.

"Wealth gained by dishonesty <u>will dwindle</u>, but whoever gathers money little by little makes it grow."[18]

This saying makes me think of the billionaire Warren Buffet who seemed to have an uncanny wisdom as far as making investments but was also a very humble people person. Warren Buffet ate at the buffet of life because he treated people right and did things right. Simple concept but profound isn't it.

Chapter 5

The Eight Secrets of Effective Entrepreneurial Thinking

Now we are going to focus on some of the key ingredients to Effective Entrepreneurial Action, which is first obtained by Effective Entrepreneurial thinking.

Words that we can begin with are: <u>Commitment</u>, <u>Ownership</u>, <u>Diligence</u>, <u>Stamina</u>, and <u>Focus</u>. Let's begin again with definitions.

Commitment- The state or quality of being dedicated to a cause. The trait of sincere and steadfast fixity of purpose. [19]

What we can see with this is that a commitment has to do with making a decision that could mean an involvement of a block of your time and this involvement could continue over a long period of time before actually accomplishing success. You want to go into your endeavor already knowing this, before you begin. (The IRS knows that most businesses take 3-5 years before they move out of the red, which means being in debt).

When I joined the Navy in my late teens I knew when I raised my hand to be sworn in that I had just committed myself to them for the next four years. I knew ahead of time before I started. I knew they essentially owned me and my time. The same thing occurred when I decided to write my first book. I knew I was in all the way. The same thing occurred when I started my first business. The same thing happened when I got married.

Since the word dedicated was used in commitment's definition, let's look at this one as well.

Dedication- Wholly committed to a course of thought or action. Devoted to a cause, ideal or purpose. [20]

No half stepping here, no skimping on the family recipe, but you're in it for the long haul. As I heard someone say, "You have stickemtuidness." Merriam Webster defines: Stick-to-it-tiveness, as dogged perseverance. "Hmmm. This is confirmation towards something that was said previously." No tip-toeing here.

Ownership- To have or possess as property. To have control over. Responsible for oneself, independent of outside help or control. [21]

I would like to add another word here called stewardship.

Stewardship- One who manages another's property, finances, or affairs. One who is in

50

charge of the household affairs of a large estate, club, hotel, or resort. [22]

I like the word stewardship because there is an element of accountability to someone else while you are managing. The reason I like this is that while you are an owner, you sometimes can do things without accountability, which could lead to other kinds of problems with regulatory industries. In stewardship, the word rings of the same level of responsibility that an owner would have but is tempered with accountability towards someone else. Now owners can be self-accountable but that takes great discipline. Not everyone has that quality.

For instance when a business man accumulates wealth he can quickly ride that wave like the fun you might find when surfing. However, experienced surfers know that they can boom and crash so they approach it with much more focus and concern. If a business man is already tempered he will treat his wealth carefully, and will not squander it so quickly. That's why you hear stories about lottery winners spending all their money quickly, ending up back to the same place, or worse than they were before they rode the wave.

Now in contrast let's look at ownership like owning a house compared to renting a house. A renter will take care of things so far but only as much as they think they need to do, and nothing more. It's not really their house; therefore if anything seriously goes wrong with it they can always call on or rely on the owner. After all it's the owner's house. If there is a plumbing problem, it's the owner's house. The renter isn't responsible. If the electric has a problem or there is a roof and tree problem, who are you going to call? Of course, you call the owner.

The renter may keep the house clean and treat the house well or they may not. The owner however will be more sensitive to things about their house than the renter. They will put more effort into the house than the renter. They may do upgrade projects on the house that a renter will not. Why is that? It is because the owner is more invested in the house due to the fact that they own it.

A renter will do improvements or upgrades, and they usually are minor, mainly with respect to improving their convenience of living temporarily knowing they will most likely move somewhere else when the time comes. They are committed to a lease but their commitment level to the house's cause is on a lesser level as compared to the owner's commitment level to the house's cause.

The same goes with respect from being an employee as opposed to being an owner. There is nothing wrong about an employee, as there is nothing wrong about a renter. Yet, a house owner thinks differently or rather more expansively than a renter. An owner of a business thinks more expansively than an employee does as well. So it is important, once again, to move one's thinking into an owner's mindset and an owner's mentality, but to also simultaneously conduct business as if you are a steward responsible to someone else for the things placed in their charge.

By nurturing and fostering this mind set from day one, your business or endeavor will be more likely to grow and stand. A renter can just come up to the owner and say I'm done, I'm out of here. An employee can quit at the drop of a hat. A business owner, when it gets a little tough can also go ahead and quit, if they are attempting to build a business with a renter's mind set.

Now knowing that it will probably take a little more effort, and that there might not be an immediate reward in being an entrepreneur, leaves many who do "dib a dab a dos,' sticking their toes in the water, feeling the temperature so they can see if they really want to get in the pool. If one approaches any kind of business like this you might as well stop there and waste no more of your time, for it just will not succeed.

Getting something new to work and be-come established can easily take more work than usual because to set something up is tougher to do then something that is established and is rou-tinely moving already. The law of inertia says:

"Things that are at rest tend to stay at rest, while things that are in motion tend to stay in motion." [23]

So to get a new business up and running it will take commitment, and an ownership mindset regularly dunked in the cup of diligence. Diligence is a mindset that has to do with how we do things. Diligence is not the same as being hasty for if your hasty, meaning your trying to get something done fast, you'll end up cutting corners and you might very well miss something important that needs to be done, or essential towards your success. Being hasty can also lead to the mistreatment of others, as you press forward towards your own goals.

The more diligent you are, the less you will miss. Unlike hastiness, that person will be considerate towards others, while things are being done. Diligence is what lifts the mind into the groove as it breaks through its obstacles. Certain obstacles can be tougher than others to overcome, but diligence is the mindset that gives people a clear victory.

Definition of **Diligent** - carried out with care and perseverance, steady effort, hard work, concentration, meticulousness. [24]

A diligent hand will rise above others in excellence as an example, end up as a leader and in charge, and also become very prosperous. *Effective Entrepreneurial Action* incorporates the favorable and flavorful seasoning of diligence. It's like the extras that turn a regular engine into a turbo engine, or like the oxygen that is added to the rocket fuel that will get your project off the ground that you're fighting for and stay lifted. Once your project is in orbit and has overcome the forces of gravity the project or business is much easier to maintain. That is diligence and inertia working together. It creates momentum and allows others to follow in its wake.

Once momentum is established it takes stamina to maintain it.

Definition of **Stamina**- Great physical or mental strength that allows you to continue doing something for a long time. Staying power, the ability to sustain and maintain, endurance, tenacity. [25], [26]

As a marathon runner is different than a sprinter, so an effective entrepreneur knows how to budget his energy, is aware of his boundaries and limitations, and paces himself so he can run his race to endure. Businesses survive because of their endurance and adaptability towards the changing needs of the consumer's demands.

Definition of **Focus** - To adjust one's vision so as to render a clear and distinct image. To concentrate energy or attention. [27]

Definition of **Concentration** - Exclusive attention to one object; close mental application. [28], [29]

The reason why we break up our long range dreams into smaller chunks and then create goals from them is to create a target that we can focus on. Many people have trouble with making their goals because they create accountability for themselves, which they may not necessarily want. They unconsciously shy away from them because they are uncomfortable. However once you extract your goals from your dreams you have concretely established stepping stones to focus in on your victory itinerary.

You now have a way to measure progress. You now have things to focus on while focusing away from the things that distract you or prevent you from obtaining what you've purposed in your heart. If you don't make your goal but make just 75% of it, or 50% of it, or even 25%, you still are making progress, so your goals do actually help you to focus.

Some people make a 30 day, 60 day, and 90 day goal list, and then go ahead to include their longer range goals of 1 year, 2 year, and 5 years for the shorter goals to sit within. If you add your investment cost to these goals it gives you a true perspective of what it will take to make it towards your final destination, and each step along the way.

I once won a free seminar by Franklin Covey via a radio station and that's where I learned the value of goal setting. Once I learned the system, I would love to set up my to-do list. When I accomplished something on my list I checked it off. I found I got about 1 $^{1/2}$ more times things done and got an energy boost as I checked those things off to boot. It became a game for me to see what I could finish throughout the day. I became more efficient.

Now it is one thing to reach your goals as an individual, but to achieve great things you will need the help of others, you will need to work with a team. This leads us to the next section, in which we will be learning how to think like a CEO, like an Executive. Once you think like an executive, you will begin to act like an executive. What things can you think of right now that you think an executive needs to have in his personal repertoire arsenal to make him a skillful executive, one that others would willingly look up to?

Take a few minutes, before moving on to the next chapter, and jot your ideas down on a piece of paper so you can see how your answers compare. You will be amazed at how much your guesses are true. This means you have the executive know how already seeded inside of you. All we have to do is cultivate it out some, and bring it to the surface.

Chapter 6

The Key Elements of Executive Action

When someone thinks about what makes an executive, they might think of words like: visionary, leadership, departmental management, budget conscious, communication skills, provider of training, team builder, delegation, and execution of leverage. You will see them sharply dressed, emanating great focus within the envelope of their entrepreneurial energy, and some, like Donald Trump, move along with their very own entourage. That is because of what they have accomplished and developed, a business conglomerate that has become very, very, big.

As far as the word vision is concerned, we have already discussed that previously, but a point that would be beneficial to add here is that executives will have already established a long term tangible track record of working at their vision and mission statement, that others can easily see. They also may have become quite wealthy and well known by this time in the process. That is because what they had started and continued to roll, snowballed upwards, turning into something huge, producing companies even on the size order of Google and Facebook and beyond.

Their personal energy and commitment towards their vision had translated, multiplied, and developed from a single car of momentum into an unstoppable fast moving **80 car train**. In Physics momentum is defined by the following equation: **$p=mv$**, which means momentum (p) = mass (m) x velocity (v). Mass is related to an objects weight and velocity is related to that object's speed. [30]

So momentum is the combined effect of the size (weight wise) of the object moving and the speed by which it moves. For example, a **ten car** train moving at **75** miles an hour has a more combined momentum contained inside of it than the same sized **ten car** train moving at **40 mph**. If a **75 mph.** train crashed it would have a greater force of impact than the **40 mph.** train would. The same would go for the comparison of two trains traveling at the same speed but having a different amount of train cars. An **85 car train** in length moving at **40 mph.** has a greater force of impact than a **10 car train in length** moving at the same speed.

Much in the same way, an entrepreneurial executive creates what's called "**business momentum**". The size of his business train is with respect to how many people that are on his team **(mass)**, that he's leading, and how fast **(velocity)** the business itself is moving towards accomplishing it's objectives. In the train example the executive is like the locomotive out in front pulling and influencing the rest of the team **(mass)**, but there is a subtle key element here that makes all of this work. It's the fact that the train's cars are ***coupled*** together. This allows the locomotive's energy to translate and distribute itself across the train and thus you have the combined momentum of the energy spread throughout the train's entire coupled mass. What a powerhouse!

A good way to see how this unstoppable train like momentum can build up is when you look at professional team sports like football, basketball, or even baseball. When a team is not doing well, not working together well, and not coupled well, the combined team energy, when competing against other teams doesn't seem to obtain victory very much. When a team has their skills honed, is working together, and has developed a combined energy amongst themselves, their energy synergizes into an even greater team momentum.

A team of ten now well united will match the output of 15-20 individuals who are not so united. In addition, this elevated team's momentum seems to knock down now every obstacle that comes into its path. That is because the team train has been coupled. Therefore the locomotive leader or coach of this train has effectively leveraged the teams' willful agreement, their energy and their talents towards the accomplishment of his vision, rather ***their*** vision.

How does he do this? An overpowering and belittling boss won't get very far, yet an encouraging and inspiring boss will. If he's really good at it, people will look to him not as their boss but instead as their leader, whom they want to work with and emulate. For the leader, it will take passion, a servant's mindset, trust, developed communication skills, and the ability to genuinely inspire hope. He is seen as both committed and ethically driven to do right. *This is how you **get** the train cars to couple and stay coupled.*

If an executive entrepreneur has motives that are differently perceived by others, and does not treat his people right, it can have a disrupting effect to the executive's intended momentum and plans. It may inadvertently set his team in disarray creating disillusionment, a further disheartening and finally he can lose many of his people. Other things can cause this dampening effect to the company's momentum as well; like if the heads or leaders under him are not truly united with him, but instead they seek to carry out their own purposes. Division and distrust will disrupt the flow, but unity and trust will cause it to grow.

For example, if a truck driver who has a heart condition, where his supervisors were not sensitive to his needs but instead sent him out for duty for long hours would not be good. Eventually the truck driver did not show up for a few days and when he came back he spoke with the big boss, the executive, and the executive then straightened the matter out with the supervisors. The concerned executive made sure that this worker got what he needed so he would not lose him. The supervisors were corrected and put back on track. Their selfishness and insensitivity to the executive's mission and vision disrupted the overall business plan and team's work flow.

So the key to effective delegation is the continued development of trust, genuine commitment displayed on behalf of the leader towards his vision or dream, along with his people that are working with him to accomplish that dream. If an executive accomplishes this super gluing effect amongst his people the train cars get coupled and the willful agreed upon momentum begins and then it just grows and grows and grows. An executive does not look to please everybody but looks to inspire, leading first by his personal example.

As the executive develops this agreed upon momentum his leverage and ability to delegate accelerates. *Trust* again is what's causing this. People, many times are more than happy to help someone's cause if they see the other person is genuine. So the translation of business energy successfully occurs when trust is carefully nurtured and developed by the leader. As John Maxwell put in his book, The Five Levels of Leadership, "People don't leave companies, people leave people."[31]

The next thing in this momentous up-building of the delegation process is the executive's training of his primary leaders. The trust has built up such that the executive can now transfer autonomous leadership and authority, which will free him, leverage wise, away from his leaders. Not to truly go away, because he will always interact and lead his leaders, but now it's more done in an injected energy fashion. This makes it so he himself can apply himself to other building activities or start new projects. If you can walk away from your business machine, and it still runs, with or without you, then you have arrived at true leverage.

An executive will treat people themselves as potentially powerful assets to be nourished and developed. With this accomplished a people asset can then be ***properly*** and **effectively** leveraged upon and the business will grow. There is a right way to do everything.

At the same time the executive will look to find new qualified people to work with, not just anybody with any attitude. He needs a good accounting department, a good lawyer or lawyers, good office managers, and the list goes on and on according to the corporation's needs. Yes, by now the business itself has probably been already incorporated. So it's a balance between finding new people licensed or complete with already developed skills, and the training of and developing the people that you already have. Of course you could train people from scratch. That can work too, but it's easier to train a squirrel to climb trees than it is to train a duck.

You as an executive can train the corporation as a whole, or you can also get into the trenches yourself with your people at times to find out how they are thinking, where they are at, and what could be done to improve their situation, and you train your leaders to train. This is part of that delegation process, for if your leaders get it and can train like you train, at least as far as the main objectives that you seek, then the more you as the executive can walk away.

That's how restaurant, store, or franchise owners operate. They start up one location, then go start another, and then another. They are now leveraging off of several businesses at the same time. It takes a lot of hard work, dedication, and perseverance, but in the end the rewards are great too.

Chapter 7
Exciting Post
Executive Activities

Now here comes the fun part. We already know that a business executive has found ways to incorporate business meetings with pleasure through paid vacations and events that are legitimately deductible at the same time. We know that it is part of the tax code and meant for businesses to do so. Therefore why not have some fun while you're at it, doing your business and have it deducted at the same time. An employee has to use his after tax money to go on vacation straight up with no deduction, whereas a business owner if done legitimately can go on vacation with money before the income is taxed.

Yet this is not the real fun I am talking about. The real fun begins when you learn to go beyond business itself to build assets. Robert Kiyosaki has defined a true asset to be something that puts "income or money" in your pocket. This asset would then generate cash flow positively on a regular basis, and the way it would be generated would be passively. By passively it is meant that the more one can walk away from the business activity or the less you need to be actually present for the business to generate its income, the more that the income generated by the business activity has become passive income. [32]

Amazingly, positive cash flow principles have existed thousands of years before books like *Think and grow Rich* and *The Secret* ever existed. I found two great examples of leverage with King Solomon, who was considered to be one of the wisest men to live on the earth, blessed with great wealth in his day.

For one, he went on a joint business venture with another King called Hiram who knew Solomon's father named King David, as a friend. King Solomon had ships built and the two entrepreneurs had sent crews to go out on sea excursions to the effect where they brought back gold, spices, jewels and other commodities, including monkeys each contributing towards a great deal of cash flow. He also received gifts from surrounding nations, for people were attracted and came for miles around to hear his unique words of wisdom and what he had to say. [33] People, basically were paying Solomon just to hear him speak. To cause that level of attraction and magnetism Solomon had to emanate things out of himself that no one else knew. There was something of value that was seen within him.

In the book, *The Song of Solomon*, a book about romance and love, you'll find in the last chapter where Solomon broke up into pieces land that he owned. He then rented those same individual pieces out to tenants. The renter's themselves then went forth and created their own businesses from their obtained parcel of land, utilizing the space to grow vineyards. Solomon here was leveraging off of the *other people's money*, who themselves were entrepreneurial business owners creating their own cash positive flow.

Through his wisdom, Solomon established a network of multi-positive cash flow assets, because each piece of land had its own positive cash flow being generated for him. This was all going on relatively in the same time frame as the joint venture sea business was occurring. He also had a business in trading chariots and horses. [34]

Once you begin to build a positive cash flow into your life, you can use that cash flow to generate new cash flow into multiple streams like Solomon did. Solomon was diligent because he went at once taking his five talents and multiplying them into five talents more. Not just individual personal talents, (which is still good because you are your own asset), but he developed multiple ways that different income would stream in.

There are many investment vehicles types that one can choose from, as far as placing the money that you have free to invest into another asset that will bring a new kind of cash flow. If you add the cash flow producing assets together: $A + B + C + D + E + F + G +$ etc., they may appear small by themselves individually, but when added together they can become quite a substantial figure. This is as far as monthly and yearly new income. Warren Buffet has purchased multiple businesses in fact doing just this.

If all of those assets were real estate the combined effect could take care of your personal living expenses easily with you no longer needing to lift a finger. If A= $250, B=$500, C=$300, D=$250, F=$650, G=350, your *additional* monthly income would be $2300. This is not including the etc. amount.

While this starter amount of passive cash flow assets may not be enough for you to travel the world expense free, all the time, it would certainly take care of many of your bills like the house payment, the car payment, along with a few others things. Each asset puzzle piece accumulates and works together, defining your overall financial picture, your monetary mosaic, and again, the etc. still has not been included.

The investments that you place into your portfolio do not have to all be in Real Estate. The point here is to keep adding to your asset portfolio whether they are people assets, real estate assets, business assets, paper assets, or other assets. Applying this long term strategy, in a step by step fashion, (wealth being gathered little by little), will soon cause your net worth to become quite large. Becoming wealthy does not happen through get rich quick schemes but it requires patience and consistency.

Asset upon asset building is what the well to do people focus on and that is how most well to do's get there. They keep building their income that is coming in, while simultaneously concentrate on reducing what flows out. This includes primarily what they pay in taxes. How can billionaires or millionaires pay less % in taxes compared to the middle class? Sounds impossible and unfair but they do. It is because they are aware or have someone making them aware of how to reduce their overall tax liability. It does not necessarily mean that they are greedy, what it does mean is that they put out the effort to become personally educated about these things so they can put their situations in order and aright.

Greediness is a matter of where someone is in their heart, it is not defined by someone's actions alone. Building up or amassing money and assets just allows you to do more things. If your personal focus is just on living it up and building self then you might have a case to say that this one might be greedy or super-selfish based on this or that. Yet, if what was in your heart you was that you wanted to build a hospital in certain places where need is, or schools, or build up entire villages would that be considered greedy then? Assets and money is not where the problem is with respect to greediness, it's where one's heart is, and this can occur with or without the money.

Money itself does not make one greedy or evil, but the *love of money* does. That is an extremely important distinction. Now can having money itself become a negative influence for you? Yes it can, *if* you let your mind influence you in that way. It is up to the individual, what happens, what they personally will allow to go on in their mind.

The Bernard Madoff scandal [35] is a good example of someone allowing greed to overtake him. Somewhere along the line he chose to listen to thoughts influencing him to decide to do what he did. It probably started out small in that he began to skim money *made off* from others unawares, but then as he became more confident in his actions it grew into something much worse.

I am not saying this to condemn him or his family, for I am sure they have already suffered greatly from the consequences of his actions. What I am saying is that lessons learned like these are good to keep in the front of your mind so you won't exchange your personal morals off for the sake of making a few more dollars. It could simply show up in the way your treating people or how your pride makes you look down upon others inwardly. Greed can express itself in many and various forms.

Having said these things about greed as a caveat, we can now move on to talk about one of the coolest ways to accelerate your asset building.

Chapter 8

Why not build yourself a Bank?

Why would you build a bank? That sounds outrageous does it not? Yet, there are people in the know who are doing just that with their own personal finances. So how does one do something like this? Don't you have to get registered, get a bank charter, licenses, etc.? Yes, you do if you if you go down the traditional path. So if it's not the traditional path, and not a traditional bank, then what is it?

Exciting concept, yes it is. To understand how this would work for you, what is your guess, as to what we need to understand first before we can build a bank for ourselves? If you guessed right, you would need to find out more clearly how a bank operates, and what is it really doing. Then after that, we can look at how to apply what the banks are doing, and discovering how we can make this happen for ourselves. Stay with me through this process. At first it might seem a little intimidating, but when you understand it you should be not only amazed, but you should see how valuable this could be for you.

So let's look at how a bank works. As I said before, the Federal Reserve interacts with our government with loans going in both directions through different investment vehicles. The Federal Reserve also interacts with the huge banks at lending and receiving money. This establishes the discount rate and the prime rate. Then these mega-banks lend to the medium and smaller banks at interest rates, which are set higher than the prime rate.

Then the banks that we do business with will also receive money in the form of deposits towards savings. While we are saving, the banks have to pay us a small interest amount. This interest rate is minimal compared to what banks were paying in saving accounts many years ago. You might get some better interest return by investing in a CD. Yet that is probably still < 2%.

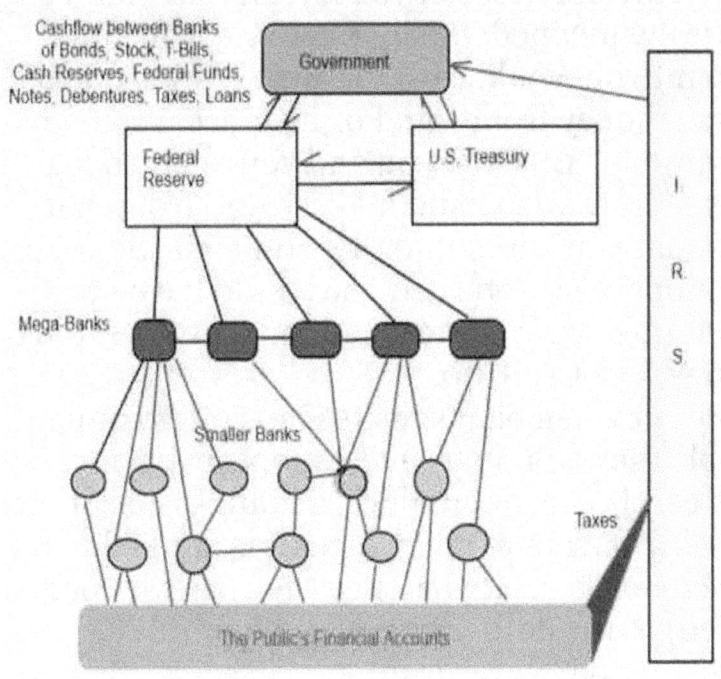

Cashflow between Banks
of Bonds, Stock, T-Bills,
Cash Reserves, Federal Funds,
Notes, Debentures, Taxes, Loans

Government

Federal
Reserve

U.S. Treasury

I.

R.

S.

Mega-Banks

Smaller Banks

Taxes

The Public's Financial Accounts

Example Model

Mechanism of the U.S Economy's Financial controls
How Banks interact through Cash, Reserves, Loans, and the Setting of Interest.

Now for those of you not all that mathematically inclined, the interest rate is the total amount you would earn in a year if someone borrowed money from you. For instance if someone borrowed $100 from you and you charged a 2% interest rate you would make $2.00 from that loan that you lent out to that someone. So when the money was returned you would have now $102. Interest is the fee paid for renting a sum of money, like the $100.

Yet when banks make loans out to other people they will then collect monthly payments on a car, home, or credit card loan. Inside of the monthly payment a portion of it is applied to the principle (The actual money the borrower borrowed), and another part of the monthly payment goes towards interest (The fee paid for renting the money). If you have outstanding loans going on in your own life, then you should be aware that most loans are front loaded, meaning you are paying more towards interest up front and less towards the principle in the beginning of the loan. As time goes on, the principle part paid and the interest part paid will equalize in percentage, and then eventually as you continue towards the end of the loan you pay on the principle more. This is the way banks make sure that they get most of their payment, even if the borrower later ends up defaulting the loan later.

So to recap, banks make money by taking in deposits from people. The interest paid from the bank to them is minimal compared to the loans that the bank structures and loans out to other people buying cars, homes, credit cards, etc. The range of interest charged goes from 2.5% all the way up into the 20+%. Think about now what your interest rate is on your car or house. That is the amount you will pay back in finance costs to the bank for borrowing that money in order to get what you purchased. So if the banks are paying interest on money deposited at <2% and obtaining money via 2.5% - 28% loans, can you see how they make money?

Yet, they don't just make money through interest, but compounded interest too. In order to understand this better let's flip the situation around. Instead of you paying interest to the bank, let's say the bank was paying interest to you on your deposit of $100,000. Let's also establish that the interest rate paid by the bank to you is at 5%. Each year you get paid $5000.00 on that $100,000 savings balance, which is what 5% of $100,000 actually calculates out to be. This applies here only if you were paid the interest straight up. Hopefully you are with me so far.

If instead however, we compound the interest yearly instead of straight up interest we would do it this way. You still get the $5,000 the first year on your $100,000 deposit in savings. At the end of the year your new balance on this money is $105,000. This is just adding $5000 (interest earned) to the original $100,000. So now since your new balance is $105,000, the next year you would be paid 5% interest on the new amount. The interest earned on $105,000 is $5,250. For year 3 it would be 5% interest paid on ($105,000 +$5,250 = $110,250). The interest paid here on $110,250 is $5,512. Your balance now is $115,762.50. The straight up 5% interest amount for the same three year timeframe would be only $115,000. The difference for just 3 years of compounded interest compared to straight up interest is ($115,762.50 - $115,000 = $762.50). It may seem small but the compounding interest is just getting started.

At 20-30 year mark point the difference between the compounding interest and regular straight up interest is huge. Most who had these investments going on would be millionaires. The compounding increases faster and faster the more rounds of compounding occur. Here is a question for you. If you doubled a penny for 30 days would you take amount resulting from this or take one million dollars today instead? Try calculating this yourself and watch how for about 2/3 of the penny doubling, it doesn't look like so much, but after that watch out. My answer that I calculated was over $10,000,000.

Go ahead and get a calculator and do this. It's very important you see this with your own eyes. Start with 1 as your penny. Then add one, which would be two pennies. That would be 1 penny doubled. That would count for day 1. Every day thereafter multiply your result by two. At the end of this divide your final result by 100, because you started with 1 penny and dividing by 100 converts your answer to dollars.

Compounding interest works in the same fashion in that its growth accelerates over time, especially the longer it's at compounding. While it may appear that banks are not really into giving out loans, they really are, because this is how they make their money. The reason why a bank will balk at someone is with respect to a person's credit score. This, of course, is the reflection of a person's payment history and how they have paid their loans in the past.

The other thing that loan officers of banks will look at is the *debt to income ratio*, [36] which boils down to the percentage of how much of the applicant's money is tied up in bills and loans already with respect to the applicant's overall income. This is how they can tell if a person can handle the requested loan. If they believe you can handle the loan they will loan out the money. This rings very true with car dealerships. They are into it for the business, as this will produce a positive cash flow for the bank and a handsome commission for the salesman involved.

Yet, if enough loans are saddled on a person, the family may begin to feel weighed down, because originally they thought it was a good idea. The new financial burden can take its toll. I came to realize that it was very important to make sure that I know that I personally can take on the extra financial burden for real before signing any contract. By doing this I protect myself in the long run.

Many people have fall into this subtle trap, and the sales force knows this. The pattern that most people follow is that when we make more income, as we get promoted or change jobs, we should be careful about the new money, using it to ease our financial burdens, but instead of saving more to give ourselves more financial room we tend to buy more things and better things with our extra money. Along with this, we tend to saddle ourselves with new loans creating an even greater liability. We do this by going out and buying that new car, or that new furniture set, or that new vacation package we've long been waiting for. This explains why someone who is making very good money, such as $200k per year, can still be living paycheck to paycheck.

Why is that do you think? It is because most people have not received much training or education on handling their personal finances properly. We self-train and wing it in a lot of ways. We can be like big kids with our money with no concept of budget and management. We spend as much as we can spend until the next paycheck, and then do it again. Our bills become just what we have to do to. Not everyone manages their income like this but there are plenty that do.

If we just had a different focus about our money many of us would do things differently and end up saving more, building up our financial situation more. If we understood better we would consciously build up our bank accounts so we could lend to ourselves and live off the interest alone. The trouble with this is the banks are paying out less than 1% interest for savings. This does not gives us much of an incentive to save, but with all of those sales going on out there, we have instead a lot of incentive to spend.

Wouldn't it be better if you could go into life with the mentality I'm going to save, save, save and then lend to myself my own loans and pay myself back. For instance, if I had amassed $100,000 I could lend myself $25,000 to purchase a car outright and then pay myself back say $300.00 per month over time which would not only recapture my income, but add to it as the $300.00 would have an extra $50.00 of it paying towards interest, yet to myself. It sounds like fantasy land but hear me out.

If this loan turned out to be a 60 month loan then I would increase my bank amount by (60 x $50 which is $3000.00), which would be added to my $100,000. Yet like a depositor in a bank, I'm also depositing more savings to myself at the same time. So the loan payments to myself are increasing my cash flow and my net worth, along with the additional continued deposits. That's how banks make their money. Why can we not follow this pattern in our own finances? Yes, it would take some discipline for some, but there are people out there doing the same thing in a different form, by saving up to buy something in cash instead of using credit. The creation of your own personal bank with your own savings is much like that.

Yet, entrepreneurs don't just save money, make money, and build up income for themselves, rather they invest their income that they've built up towards other new assets aimed at bringing in even more positive cash flow. They take their $25,000 and instead of buying a car they put that $25,000 down into a business or real estate property or other positive cash flow producing vehicle, then allow other people (renters) to pay them with their money, so as to pay their own asset loan back. The incoming new cash flow can even be structured so that both loans are paid for, the original $25,000 loan any leftover mortgage amount on the real estate that you purchased, or at least most of it.

The point being is that if other people are paying off your positive cash flow asset, you are now building your asset base and net worth even faster. You eventually might need to open up more bank accounts just to handle the income, as you purchase more positive cash flow financial vehicles that build up your own bank's balance. Your money is essentially working better and accruing in more than one place at the same time.

Yet some of you might be saying, well that sounds all well and good but I don't have my bank account built up yet and I am just a humble employee working my 40-50 hours. Or you might say, you don't have the self-discipline to save up like this, besides the fact is that you have bills to pay. I would answer you and say, "I know", and the banks and salesman know this to, and that's why we've been all tied up, but there still is a ray of hope.

Most investment vehicles bring cash flow via three categories. They are either taxed now, taxed later (like 401k's), or taxed exempt. Which category would you prefer? I am assuming you prefer the tax never category. If so, an investment vehicle like the Roth IRA or the 7702 can create this pseudo-bank for yourself inside of it.

The 7702 is a tax code provision that many have not heard of. It allows three things to occur. One, it allows you to create your own bank inside of it because this particular financial vehicle will allow you to take loans against your principle, and in some instances at a minimal interest. I know of one investment vehicle that eventually allows you to take loans to yourself at 0.0% interest! Secondly, it also allows you to plan for retirement simultaneously. Thirdly, it makes provision for you to pass income on to your children or beneficiary as the 7702 is a specialized life insurance vehicle that allows all three of these things to occur.

Many wealthy people use these vehicles all the time, along with other investment vehicles in their portfolio. What it means for the rest of us is that we can set up these vehicles, while we are young and healthy and keep adding to this tax-free vehicle, as opposed to a 401k which is taxed at the end when we take it out. What's really happening there is the tax is being taking out from the harvest money rather than the seed money. If I am to be taxed, I would rather be taxed off of a $3000.00 rather than $300,000.

Instead of us going out and spending all our money away, getting taxed while we earn, getting taxed while we spend, and paying interest to others, why not take some of that money and use it to invest in our own future, thinking long range, preparing for retirement, and creating a bank where we can loan to ourselves at the same time. When we do this and purchase new assets we can quickly snowball financial momentum.

If you incorporate a financial strategy like this you will have more than enough for the things you need and you will be able to take loans out for those things when you need them. By the way you can purchase multiple 7702s, and if you cannot do it for yourself you still can get one for your children, as you the owner get the loan advantages while you still own it. These 7702s come in different sizes and some are very flexible and include a guaranteed return on your investment.

If I was 20-35 years old and starting out in life, I would start out by putting money into a 7702, find one that's flexible, one that has great loan provisions and then find a way to start a business whether it's home based or not so I could reduce my tax liability. I would then find ways to purchase positive cash flow assets by the time I was 40-50. I would be set for both my present and the future even in this shaky economy. Because I educated myself financially, I would even know where to park my assets, where they would be relatively safe, even if there was a global economic failure. (If I could not I would set up one for each of my children but I would be the owner and still retain the rights of the bank like loan provision until I passed it to them).

How could that be? Because even during the worst of financial times, like during the 1929 market crash, there were those companies that seemed unaffected, even benefitting from the collapse. Just think about if the value of everything around you went down to next to nothing like houses or land and you just happened to have your wealth protected, parked, and available to then go buy these next to nothing items.

If one prepares wisely, gathering little by little, one can weather the storm and come out perhaps even better than when you were before. It's really all about the way you look at things.

As a man thinks, so is he.

Chapter 9

The End, or should I say, The Beginning

Now we have covered a lot of ground here. There is a lot for you to think about. We have gone from how people see things, as far as their dreams. We have discussed how to have a proper entrepreneurial mindset when looking at starting a business. We have spoken on why it's important for one to start a business of their own, to open the door for tax liability reduction, and to create greater chances to build income. We have generally discussed how banks work, how taxes work, and how the economy works.

We have laid out a pathway for you to understand what is required to take effective action as an entrepreneur and even an executive. We have shown you how to begin building your own financial system through the taking advantage of the means and financial vehicles out there to create a personal snowballing asset base building of your own positive cash flow economy, within a shaky one.

The reason why I am doing what I am doing is not to just build up my personal financial empire, but I am looking to solve some problems in Haiti and Dominican Republic. I visited Haiti when I was in my twenty's and was devastated by what I saw there. The poverty there really pricked my heart. Since then, they have had that giant earthquake. I haven't been there lately, but I can imagine what it is like for them.

If I can help change a few people's lives there, I will certainly do so. Like that story where the young boy was tossing starfish back in the ocean, and an older man came up to him and said, "Why are you doing what you're doing?" The boy responded, "I am trying to save them." The man said, "But you know that you can't save them all, most of them will die, so this is a total a waste of your time." The boy responded back, "I know, but I can save some, even if I do it one at a time." 37

Whatever you do in your endeavors, never stop finding ways to be of benefit to others. For as you build your assets, the greatest asset is you. In that you can become an asset for someone else's benefit. Don't worry, you won't lose, "For the measure you give, will be the measure you get!" 38 I am not saying here to give it all away but what I am saying is that as you give to others, your own personal situation will accelerate and increase.

How do I know this? It is because a King, named Solomon, said this particular proverb:

"Some people give freely and gain more; others refuse to give and end up with less."

Give freely and you will profit, help others and you will gain more for yourself.

Solomon knew the secret of genuine prosperity. For true gain is not what you can just gain for yourself, rather true gain is the expansion of your ability be of service to others. If you serve only yourself, perhaps a few family members and a friend or two, then you are limited to that world, flowing like a brook, or a small tributary. If you attribute yourself to something greater than your flow may become the size of a mighty river. If that is the case then your cash flow, which will substantiate your dreams, will flow mighty as well.

Bibliography

1. .
http://www.richmondfed.org/faqs/frs/

2. .
http://www.federalreserve.gov/monetarypolicy/
openmarket.htm

3. .
http://www.federalreserve.gov/faqs/credit_1284
6.htm

4. .
http://en.wikipedia.org/wiki/Consumer_price_i
ndex

5. .Bible, Proverbs 13:12 (NKJV)

6. . Bible, Habakkuk 2:2 (KJV)

7. . Think and Grow Rich, Napoleon
Hill, Ralston Society, pg 53

8. . Bible, Proverbs 13:19 (ESV)

9. .
http://en.wikipedia.org/wiki/Robert_Kiyosaki

10. . http://www.merriam-webster.com/dictionary/entitlement

11. . https://www.stephencovey.com/7habits/7habits-habit1.php

12. . http://www.richdad.com/Resources/Rich-Dad-Financial-Education-Blog/September-2012/How-Can-I-Afford-That.aspx

13. . Bible, Proverbs 23:7 KJV

   a) Tax code length: http://www.fourmilab.ch/uscode/26usc/

14. . http://www.thefreedictionary.com/Effective

15. . http://dictionary.reference.com/browse/efficient

16. . http://www.thefreedictionary.com/ethics

17. . http://www.biblestudytools.com/2-timothy/2-5-compare.html

18. . http://www.biblegateway.com/passage/?search=Proverbs%2013.11&version=NKJV

19. .
https://www.google.com/#q=commitment+dfini
tion

20. .
http://www.thefreedictionary.com/dedicate

21. . http://legal-
dictionary.thefreedictionary.com/owner

22. . http://www.merriam-
webster.com/dictionary/stewardship

23. .
http://en.wikipedia.org/wiki/Newton's_laws_of
_motion

24. .
http://www.thefreedictionary.com/diligent

25. .
http://www.thefreedictionary.com/stamina

26. . http://www.merriam-
webster.com/dictionary/stamina

27. .
http://www.thefreedictionary.com/focus

28. .
http://www.oxforddictionaries.com/us/definitio
n/american_english/concentrate

29. .
http://www.thefreedictionary.com/concentratio
n

30. .
http://en.wikipedia.org/wiki/Momentum

31. .
http://books.google.com/books?id=geI0_auAFS
UC&pg=PT9&lpg=PT9&dq=people+don't+leave
+company+people+leave+people+john+maxwell
&source=bl&ots=rYNaODB32R&sig=ARG5ZyfJ
mopLe6kxaWv225MNOgc&hl=en&sa=X&ei=_4
RxUqvFONHwkQfQxYCY-
Ag&ved=0CFIQ6AEwBA#v=onepage&q=people
%20don't%20leave%20company%20people%20l
eave%20people%20john%20maxwell&f=false

32. .
http://en.wikipedia.org/wiki/Robert_Kiyosaki#
Financial_advice

33. . Bible, 2nd Chronicles 9:21-25

34. . Bible, 1rst Kings 10:27-29

35. .
http://en.wikipedia.org/wiki/Bernard_Madoff

36. .
http://learn.bankofamerica.com/articles/managing-credit/keeping-your-debt-load-manageable.html

37. .
http://www.goodreads.com/author/quotes/56782.Loren_Eiseley

38. . Bible, Mark 4:21-25

39. . Bible, Proverbs 11:24 (ESV)

Bibliography Ending Note:

The occasional reference to Biblical verses here in the text was to only illustrate just a few of the many verses discussing how to work with your money. The Bible does graciously provide information to the reader on many aspects in life. In fact it even goes as far as to make the bold assertion that it *pertains to all things in life.* (2nd Peter 1:3)

—————

Other Books to Read:

Think and Grow Rich -Napoleon Hill

Rich Dad, Poor Dad –Kiosaki
Cash Flow Quadrant- Kiosaki

The Seven Habits of Highly Successful People
Stephen Covey

The Eight Habit
Stephen Covey

The Power of Trust
Stephen Covey

177 Mental Toughness Secrets of the World Class
Steve Siebold

The Five Levels of Leadership
John C. Maxwell

The One Minute Millionaire
Robert G. Allen, Mark Victor Hansen

..About The Author

James Regan is presently enjoying living in San Antonio, Texas USA. He lives with his beautiful wife Miriam. He works at a Phase I Drug Research facility, is an entrepreneur, a Youth Pastor and a cofounder of an extensive Christian website

http://www.alloftheanswers.com

Most people will do the things they want to do if they just could see the way to do it. He enjoys helping people to see this way, achieve their personal dreams and is in the process of building training courses to do so in the future.

His personal website is-
http://authorjamesregan.com

www.ingramcontent.com/pod-product-compliance
Lightning Source LLC
Chambersburg PA
CBHW051735170526
45167CB00002B/946